MY FIRST
COOK
B·O·O·K

WRITTEN BY

ANGELA WILKES

ALFRED A. KNOPF 🐎 NEW YORK

Design   Roger Priddy
Photography   David Johnson
Home Economist   Dolly Meers
Editor   Jane Elliot

Dorling Kindersley would like to thank Henrietta Winthrop,
Pamela Cowan, Dan Bristow, Isobel Bulat, and
Nancy Graham for their help in producing this book.

THIS IS A BORZOI BOOK PUBLISHED BY ALFRED A. KNOPF, INC.

Copyright © 1989 by Dorling Kindersley Limited, London.
All rights reserved under International and Pan-American Copyright
Conventions. Published in the United States by Alfred A. Knopf, Inc.,
New York. Distributed by Random House, Inc., New York. Originally
published in Great Britain by Dorling Kindersley Limited, London.
Printed in Italy.

First American edition, 1989

4   6   8   10   9   7   5

Library of Congress Cataloging-in-Publication Data
Wilkes, Angela. My first cookbook. 'A Borzoi book'—T.p. verso.
Summary: Introduces the tools, recipes, and techniques necessary for
such dishes as speedy pizzas and bread bears. 1. Cookery—Juvenile
literature. [1. Cookery] I. Title. TX652.5.W55 1989
641.5'123   88-13798
ISBN 0-394-80427-9

CONTENTS

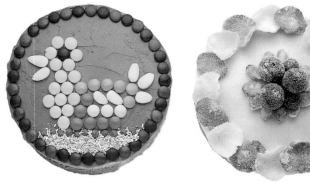

COOKING BY PICTURES

My First Cookbook shows you step-by-step how to make all sorts of delicious things to eat. Easy-to-follow recipes show you which ingredients you need, what to do with them, and what the finished food should look like – life size! Every recipe is followed by lots of colorful ideas on how to decorate what you have made. Below are the points to look for in each recipe, and on the opposite page is an important list of cook's rules to read before you start.

How to use this book

The ingredients
All the ingredients you need for each recipe are shown life-size, to help you check you have the right amounts.

Increasing the quantity
Each recipe tells you how many things the ingredients make. To make more, double or triple the quantities.

Cook's tools
These illustrated checklists show you which utensils you need to have ready before you start cooking.

SPICY COOKIES

You can make spicy cookies in all kinds of different shapes*. You can make them for parties or just for snacks. The ingredients shown here will make about twenty-five cookies. On the next four pages you can find out how to cut out and decorate your cookies. *Remember to have an adult handy for supervision while you are making this recipe.*

You will need

6 tablespoons butter

1 small egg

1¼ cups (10 oz) plain flour

¼ cup (2 oz) corn syrup

1 level teaspoon baking powder

1 tablespoon cinnamon

½ cup (4oz) soft brown sugar, packed

COOK'S TOOLS

Wooden spoon
Rolling pin
Mixing bowl
Measuring cup
Strainer
Cookie cutters
Knife
Fork
Spatula
Baking pan

Making the cookie dough

1 Preheat oven to 325°F/170°C. Sift the flour and cinnamon through the strainer into the mixing bowl, then stir in the sugar.

2 Add the butter and cut it up. Rub the flour and butter together with your fingertips until the mixture looks like breadcrumbs.

3 Break the egg into a measuring cup and beat it with a fork. Add the corn syrup and mix it with the egg until smooth.

4 Make a hollow in the flour and pour in the egg mixture. Mix everything together well until you have a big ball of dough.

5 Put the ball of dough into a plastic bag and place it in the refrigerator for 30 minutes. It will then be easier to roll out.

6 Sprinkle some flour on a table and your rolling pin. Roll out the dough evenly until it is about ¼ inch thick.

10   *For a different flavor, you can add ¼ teaspoon of other spices, such as cloves, nutmeg, or allspice – alone or in combination.

Turn the page to see what to do next. 11

Cook's rules

1. Do not cook anything unless there is an adult there to help you.

2. Read each recipe before you start, to make sure you have everything you need.

3. Wash your hands and put on an apron before you start cooking.

4. Carefully measure all the ingredients you use.

5. Always wear oven gloves when picking up anything hot, or when putting things into or taking them out of the oven.

6. Be very careful with sharp knives.

7. Turn saucepan handles to the side of the stove, so that you do not knock them.

8. Never leave the kitchen while electric or gas burners are on.

9. Always turn the oven off when you have finished cooking.

Step-by-step
Step-by-step photographs and clear instructions show you what to do at every stage of the recipe.

The oven-glove symbol
Whenever you see this symbol at the beginning of an instruction, you should ask an adult for help.

The finishing touches
Life-size pictures show you how to decorate the things you have made and which ingredients to use.

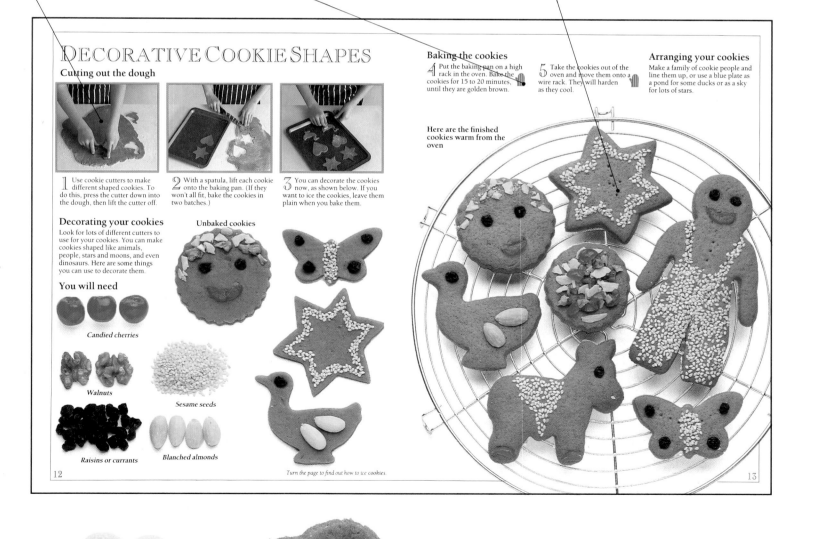

DECORATIVE COOKIE SHAPES

Cutting out the dough

1. Use cookie cutters to make different shaped cookies. To do this, press the cutter down into the dough, then lift the cutter off.

2. With a spatula, lift each cookie onto the baking pan. (If they won't all fit, bake the cookies in two batches.)

3. You can decorate the cookies now, as shown below. If you want to ice the cookies, leave them plain when you bake them.

Decorating your cookies
Look for lots of different cutters to use for your cookies. You can make cookies shaped like animals, people, stars and moons, and even dinosaurs. Here are some things you can use to decorate them.

You will need

Candied cherries

Walnuts

Sesame seeds

Raisins or currants

Blanched almonds

Unbaked cookies

Baking the cookies

4. Put the baking pan on a high rack in the oven. Bake the cookies for 15 to 20 minutes, until they are golden brown.

5. Take the cookies out of the oven and move them onto a wire rack. They will harden as they cool.

Arranging your cookies
Make a family of cookie people and line them up, or use a blue plate as a pond for some ducks or as a sky for lots of stars.

Here are the finished cookies warm from the oven

Turn the page to find out how to ice cookies.

12

13

COOK'S TOOLS

Here and on the next three pages are all the utensils you will need to follow the recipes in this book. To make it easy for you to check that you have everything you need before you start cooking, there is a checklist of cook's tools at the beginning of every recipe.

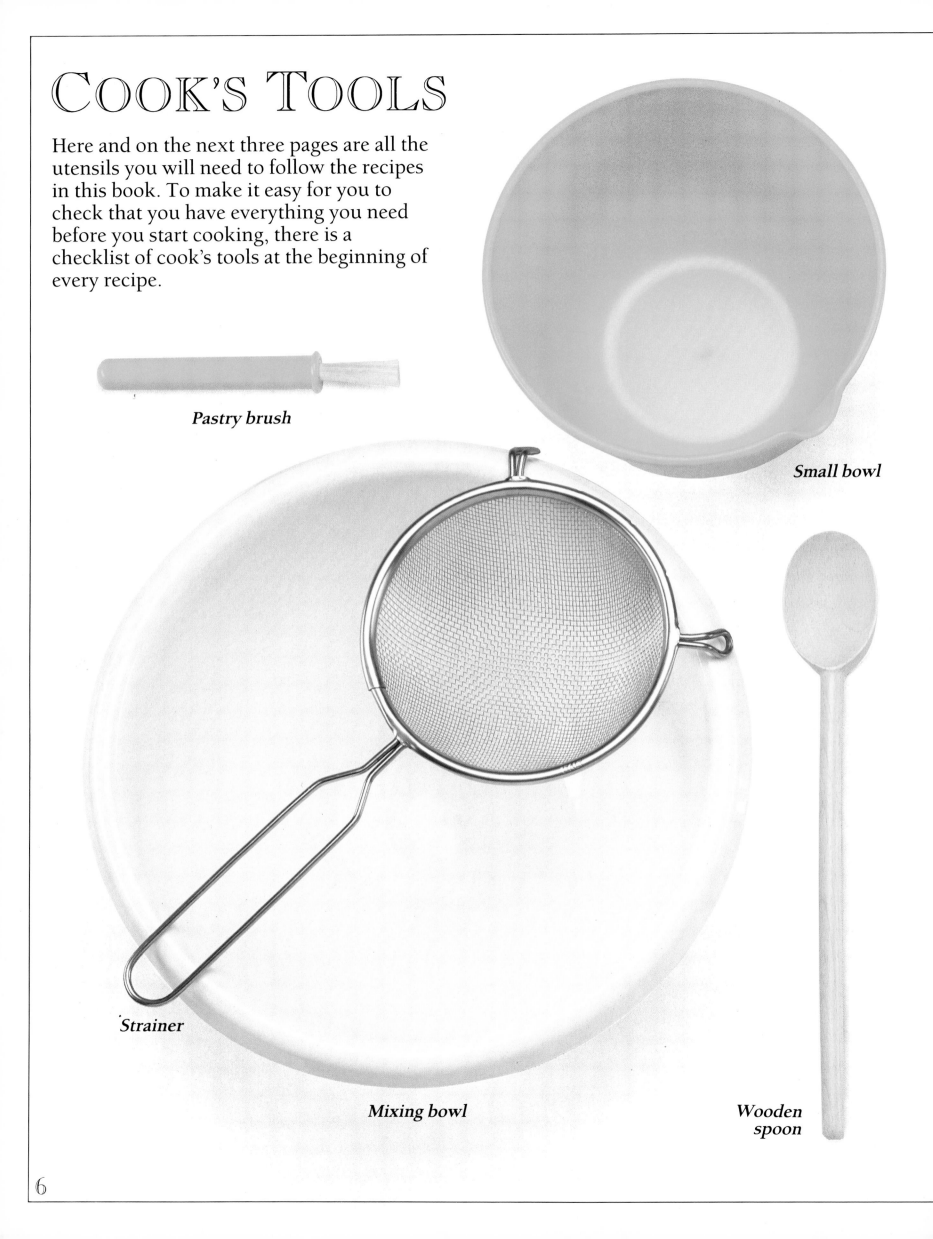

Pastry brush

Small bowl

Strainer

Mixing bowl

Wooden spoon

Chopping board   *Apron*

Rolling pin

Sharp knife

Knife

Fork

Tablespoon

Measuring cup

Teaspoon

7

MORE COOK'S TOOLS

Cheese grater

Oven glove

Wire cooling rack

2 8-inch
layer cake pans

Small saucepan

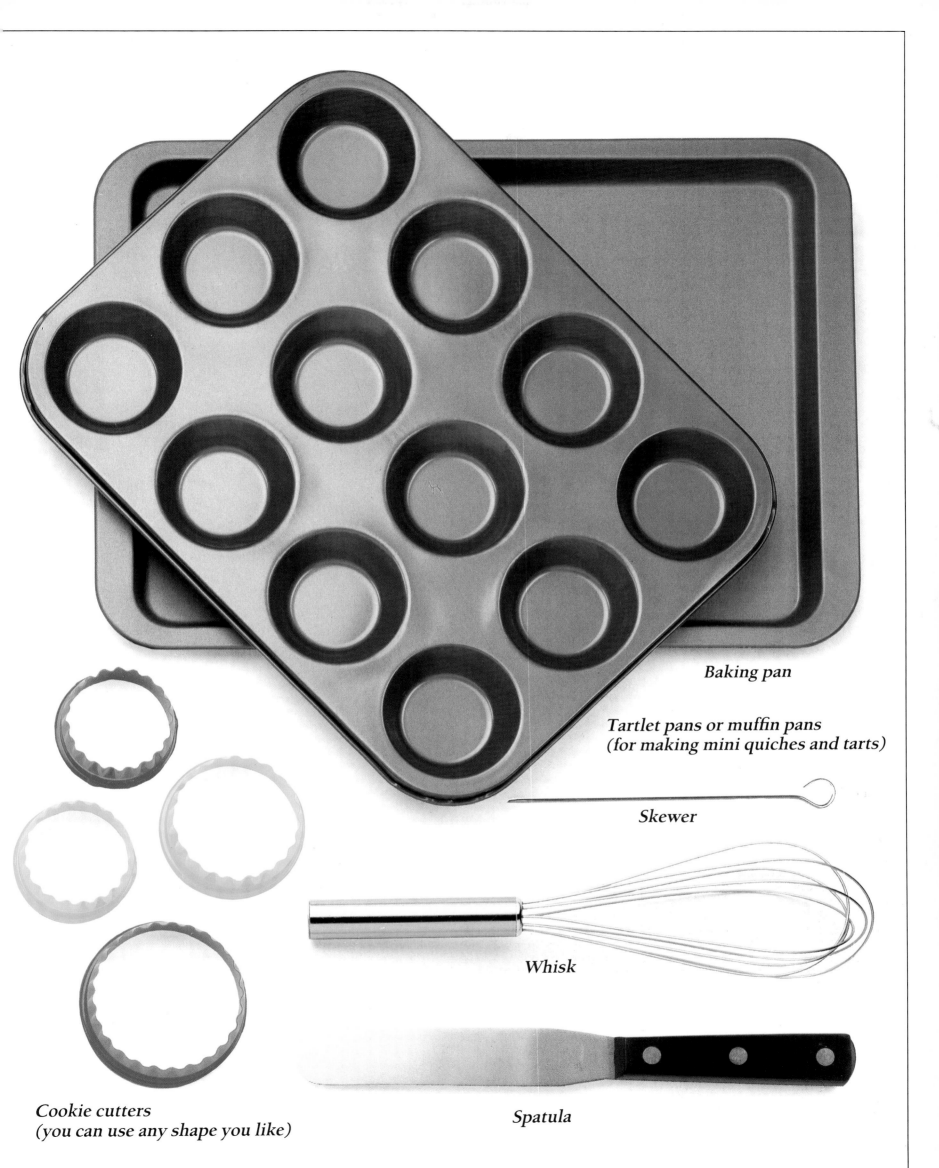

Baking pan

Tartlet pans or muffin pans
(for making mini quiches and tarts)

Skewer

Whisk

Cookie cutters
(you can use any shape you like)

Spatula

9

SPICY COOKIES

You can make spicy cookies in all kinds of different shapes*. You can make them for parties or just for snacks. The ingredients shown here will make about twenty-five cookies. On the next four pages you can find out how to cut out and decorate your cookies. *Remember to have an adult handy for supervision while you are making this recipe.*

You will need

6 tablespoons butter

1 small egg

2 cups plain flour

Making the cookie dough

1 Preheat oven to 325°F/170°C. Sift the flour, the baking powder, and the cinnamon through the strainer into the mixing bowl, then stir in the sugar.

2 Add the butter and cut it up. Rub the flour and butter together with your fingertips until the mixture looks like breadcrumbs.

3 Break the egg into a measuring cup and beat it with a fork. Add the corn syrup and mix it with the egg until smooth.

*For a different flavor, you can add ¼ teaspoon of other spices, such as cloves, nutmeg, or allspice – alone or in combination.

¼ cup (2 oz) corn syrup

1 level teaspoon
baking powder

COOK'S TOOLS

Mixing bowl

Wooden spoon

Rolling pin

Measuring cup

Strainer

Cookie
cutters

Knife

Fork

Spatula

Baking pan

1 tablespoon cinnamon

½ cup (4oz) soft brown sugar, packed

4 Make a hollow in the flour and pour in the egg mixture. Mix everything together well until you have a big ball of dough.

5 Put the ball of dough into a plastic bag and place it in the refrigerator for 30 minutes. It will then be easier to roll out.

6 Sprinkle some flour on a table and your rolling pin. Roll out the dough evenly until it is about ¼ inch thick.

Turn the page to see what to do next.

DECORATIVE COOKIE SHAPES

Cutting out the dough

1 Use cookie cutters to make different shaped cookies. To do this, press the cutter down into the dough, then lift the cutter off.

2 With a spatula, lift each cookie onto the baking pan. (If they won't all fit, bake the cookies in two batches.)

3 You can decorate the cookies now, as shown below. If you want to ice the cookies, leave them plain when you bake them.

Decorating your cookies

Look for lots of different cutters to use for your cookies. You can make cookies shaped like animals, people, stars and moons, and even dinosaurs. Here are some things you can use to decorate them.

You will need

Unbaked cookies

Candied cherries

Walnuts

Sesame seeds

Raisins or currants

Blanched almonds

12

Turn the page to find out how to ice cookies.

Baking the cookies

4 Put the baking pan on a high rack in the oven. Bake the cookies for 15 to 20 minutes, until they are golden brown.

5 Take the cookies out of the oven and move them onto a wire rack with the spatula. They will harden as they cool.

Arranging your cookies

Make a family of cookie people and line them up, or use a blue plate as a pond for some ducks or as a sky for lots of stars.

Here are the finished cookies warm from the oven

Easy Icing

To make fancier cookies you can ice them before decorating them. You must bake the cookies plain and make sure that they have cooled completely before icing them. Below you can find out how to make white icing and chocolate flavored icing.

¼ cup cocoa powder
(for chocolate icing only)

You will need

1 cup confectioners' sugar

1 tablespoon hot water

Candied cherries

Making the icing

1 Sift the sugar into the small bowl. Add the water a little at a time, mixing it with the sugar to make a smooth paste.

2 To make chocolate icing, use ½ cup sugar and the cocoa powder. Make it the same way as the white icing.

3 Spoon a little icing on each cookie and spread it out evenly with a wet knife. Don't worry if it dribbles down the edges a bit.

Decorating the cookies

4 Before the icing sets, decorate your cookies with any of the things shown below. You can make patterns on them or decorate them to look like faces or animals. Here are some ideas to try.

Chocolate chips

Candy-covered chocolates

Chocolate sprinkles

Multicolored sprinkles

ICE CREAM SUNDAES

Ice cream sundaes are great fun to make. All you need is ice cream, some sauces, and lots of tasty things to put on top. You must make sundaes very quickly, so they don't melt. Put them in the refrigerator as you finish them, or eat them at once! On the next two pages there are some ideas for making silly sundaes. *Remember to have an adult handy for supervision while you are making this recipe.*

COOK'S TOOLS

Wooden spoon

2 small bowls

Knife

Strainer

2 big spoons

Glasses or dishes

Small saucepan

You will need

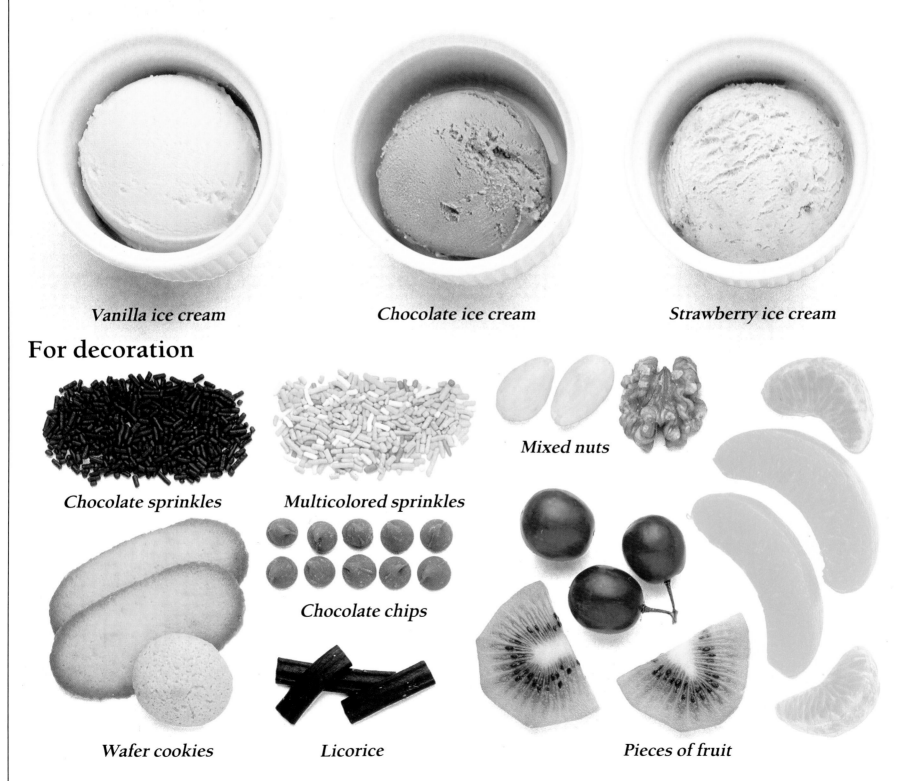

Vanilla ice cream

Chocolate ice cream

Strawberry ice cream

For decoration

Chocolate sprinkles

Multicolored sprinkles

Mixed nuts

Chocolate chips

Wafer cookies

Licorice

Pieces of fruit

Making the sauces
For raspberry sauce

¾ cup (6 oz) raspberries (frozen or fresh)

6 tablespoons (3 oz) sugar

For chocolate sauce

4 ounces dark chocolate

Raspberry sauce

1 Wash the raspberries and put them in a strainer over a bowl. Then push the raspberries through the strainer using a wooden spoon.

2 Add the sugar to the raspberry pulp a little at a time. Then stir the sauce vigorously until all the sugar has dissolved.

Chocolate sauce

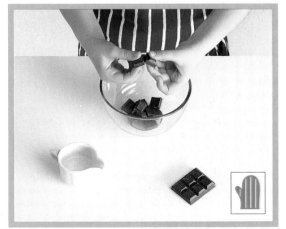

1 Break up the chocolate. Put it in a small bowl with the water. Heat some water in the saucepan until it gently bubbles.

2 Place the bowl over the saucepan until the chocolate melts. Turn off the heat and stir the chocolate until smooth.

3 tablespoons water

Now turn the page for decorating ideas.

17

SILLY SUNDAES

You can make sundaes that look like colorful insects or flowers, by using the ingredients and sauces shown on the last two pages, or you can experiment with ideas of your own. First put the ice cream in the dishes, then add the sauces, and finally the topping ingredients. You will find it easier to scoop ice cream out of containers if you use a metal spoon, dipping it into a bowl of hot water between each scoop.

BUMBLEBEE ICE CREAM

Chocolate sauce

Chocolate-chip eyes

Vanilla ice cream

Wafer-cookie wings

Sliced peaches

BUTTERFLY ICE CREAM

Chocolate-chip eyes

Almonds

Chocolate ice cream

Grapes

Sliced peaches

Licorice antennae

Chocolate and multicolored sprinkles

Chocolate chips

Sliced fresh pineapple wings

FRUITY FLOWER
(for two people)

Sliced strawberry

CATERPILLAR ICE CREAM
(for three people)

Use one scoop each of chocolate, strawberry and vanilla ice cream.

Raspberry sauce

Licorice antennae

Cherry nose

Wafer cookies

Chocolate chips

Eyes made of halved grapes

LADYBUG ICE CREAM

Raspberry sauce

Chopped nuts

Sliced kiwi fruit

Strawberry ice cream

Grape eyes

Licorice

Raspberry sauce

Strawberry ice cream

Chocolate-chip spots

CHEESY POTATO BOATS

Stuffed potatoes are a meal in themselves and are easy to make. Here are some unusual ideas on how to decorate them once you have baked them. Potatoes take a long time to bake, so put them in the oven 1 to 1½ hours before you want to eat them*. *Remember to have an adult handy for supervision while you are making this recipe.*

For two people you will need

2 pats of butter

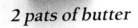
¼ cup (2 oz) shredded cheese

1 large scrubbed potato

For decoration you can use any of these things

Button mushrooms

Strips of cucumber

Pitted black olives

Carrots, sliced or cut into sticks

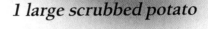
Cheese slices cut into shapes

COOK'S TOOLS

Small bowl

Knife

Fork

Tablespoon

Cheese grater

Greased baking pan

Peppers, cut into strips

Shredded lettuce

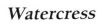
Watercress

* Ask an adult to check if the potatoes are done. Leave the oven on for step 3.

Baking the potatoes

1 Preheat the oven to 400°F/ 200°C. Prick the potatoes and place them on the greased baking pan. Bake for 1½ hours*.

2 Cut the baked potatoes in half lengthwise. Scoop the centers into the bowl and mash them. Stir in butter and shredded cheese.

3 Spoon the mixture back into the potato skins and level them off. Then put them back into the oven for another 15 minutes.

Carefully prick the potatoes using a fork or skewer.

Decorating the potatoes

You can decorate the potatoes once they have been baked a second time. Make them into sailboats, rowboats or tugboats as shown here.

STUFFED SCHOONER

Yellow pepper flag

Toothpick mast

Cheese sail

Red pepper deck

POTATO ROWBOAT

Black olives

Carrot oars

Watercress leaves

Cucumber oars

Black olives

Shredded lettuce for sea

TUGBOAT TATER

Watercress steam

Funnels made of carrot slices and mushroom stems

Red pepper

SPEEDY PIZZAS

Here you can see how to make a quick pizza and sauce, and on the next page are ideas for toppings. You can make two 4 inch pizzas from the ingredients below. *Remember to have an adult handy for supervision while you are making this recipe.*

You will need

A pinch of salt

3 tablespoons butter

3–4 tablespoons milk

¾ cup (6 oz) self-rising flour**

¼ cup (2 oz) shredded cheese

1 small onion

For the sauce

1 tablespoon tomato paste

A pinch each of salt and pepper

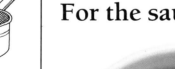

1 small can tomatoes

COOK'S TOOLS

Mixing bowl

Small saucepan

Wooden spoon

Rolling pin

Knife

Cheese grater

Sharp knife*

Cutting board

Baking pan

*Make sure that an adult helps you when you are using a sharp knife.
**Self-rising flour already contains salt and baking powder.

Making the sauce

1 Preheat the oven to 425°F/ 220°C. Peel the onion, then cut it in half and chop it up finely on the cutting board.

2 Put the chopped onion in the saucepan. Add the tomatoes, tomato paste, salt and pepper, and stir the mixture together.

3 Cook the mixture over a low heat for about 15 minutes, stirring from time to time. Then turn off the heat and let it cool.

Making the dough

1 While the sauce is cooking, make the dough. Put the flour, salt, and butter in the mixing bowl. Cut the butter into small pieces.

2 Rub the pieces of butter into the flour between your fingertips and thumbs until the mixture looks like breadcrumbs.

3 Add the shredded cheese and milk to the flour mixture. Mix everything together until you have a smooth ball of dough.

4 Divide the dough in two and make each into a ball. Roll each ball of dough into a circular shape about 4 inches across.

5 Lay the circles of dough on the greased baking pan. Spoon the tomato sauce on them, spreading it out evenly to the edges.

6 Decorate the pizzas (see next page). Put them in the oven for 15 to 20 minutes, until the edges are golden brown.

Now turn the page.

PARTY PIZZAS

Once you have made the basic pizzas – but before baking them – you can turn them into picture pizzas, using any of the ingredients below. Try making one of the pizzas shown here, or experiment with your own ideas.

Topping ingredients

Shredded cheese

Sliced ham cut into strips

Pepper strips

Pitted black olives

Cheese slices cut into shapes

Sliced sausage

ITALIAN PIZZA

Diced red pepper

Sliced cooked sausage

Diced ham

Sliced mushrooms

Corn

Sliced mushroom

Canned corn

Shredded cheese

Diced green pepper

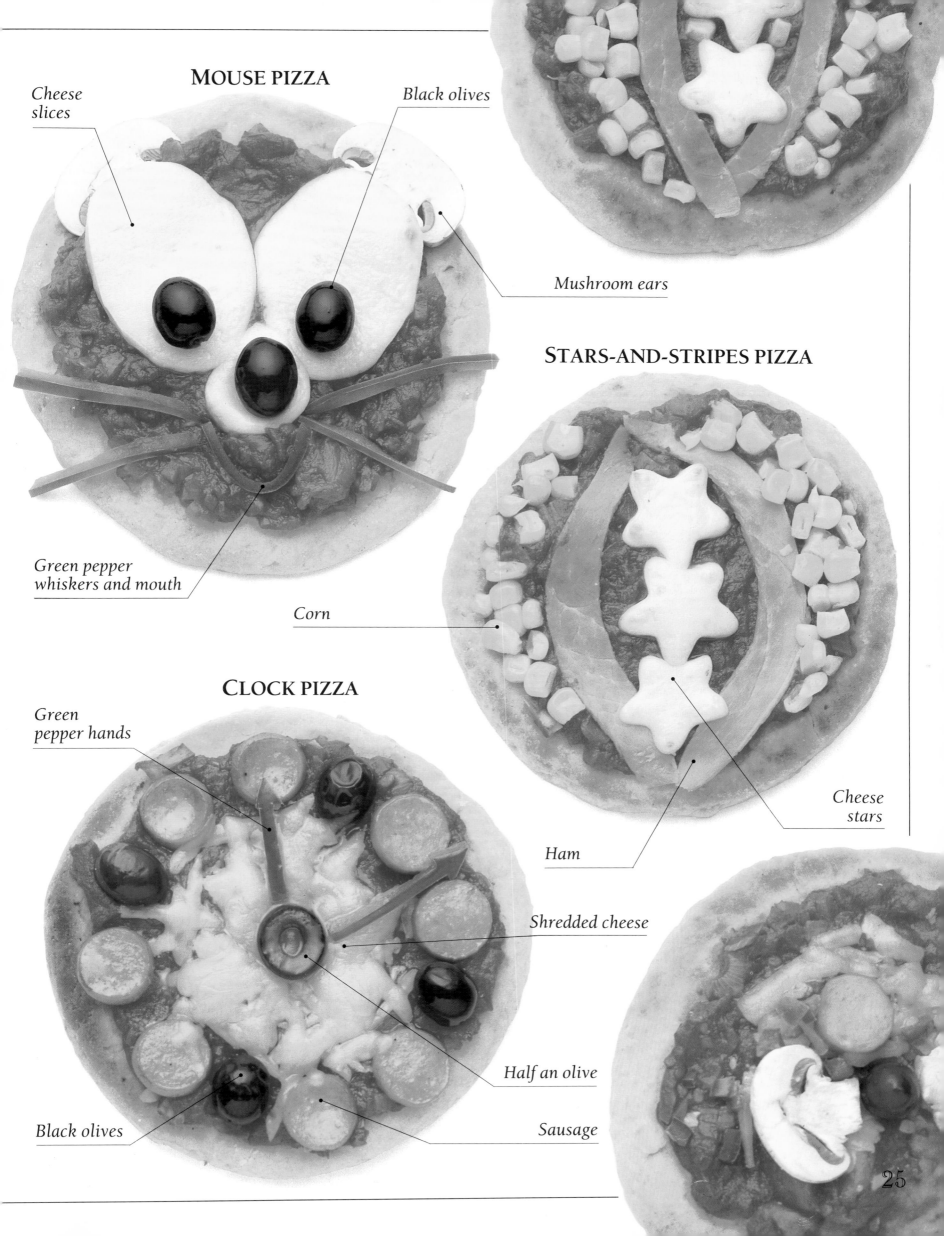

MOUSE PIZZA

Cheese slices

Black olives

Mushroom ears

Green pepper whiskers and mouth

STARS-AND-STRIPES PIZZA

Corn

Cheese stars

Ham

CLOCK PIZZA

Green pepper hands

Shredded cheese

Half an olive

Black olives

Sausage

FRUIT FOOLS

You can make fools with any fruit soft enough to mash with a fork. This recipe shows how to make strawberry or banana fools and yields four servings.* *Remember to ask an adult to supervise while you are cutting up the fruit.*

You will need

2 tablespoons (1 oz) sugar, or to taste

2 small bananas

1 cup (8 oz) yogurt

A wedge of lemon**

OR 1 cup (8 oz) strawberries

For decoration

Chocolate chips

Candied cherries

Seedless grapes

Wafer cookies

Sliced kiwi fruit

COOK'S TOOLS

Bowl

Serving dishes

Sharp knife

Fork

Whisk

Wooden spoon

*For a richer tasting dessert, try substituting whipped cream for some of the yogurt.

**A few drops of lemon juice will keep the banana fool from losing its color

26

What you do

1 Cut the strawberries in half or peel and slice the bananas. Put the fruit in the bowl and mash with a fork until smooth.

2 Whisk the yogurt until it is smooth and creamy. Add this and the sugar to the mashed fruit. Stir well.

3 Pour the fruit mixture into the serving dishes or glasses. Decorate them as shown below, or however you like.

BEAR FOOL

FOOLISH DOG

The banana fool bear has wafer ears, eyes made of cookies and chocolate chips, a cherry nose, and a slice of kiwi fruit for a mouth.

The flower pattern on this strawberry fool is made of sliced kiwi fruit and candied cherry slivers arranged around a grape in the middle.

FLOWERING FOOL

The strawberry-fool dog has sliced strawberry ears, eyes made of grapes, a cookie and chocolate chip nose, and whiskers made of kiwi fruit slivers.

QUICK BREAD

Making bread is a lot of fun. This recipe makes enough dough for eight rolls. Here you can see how to make the dough. The next two pages show you how to make and decorate the rolls. Turn to page 32 and see how to make a whole family of bears. *Remember to have an adult handy for supervision while you are making this recipe.*

You will need

½ envelope quick-acting dried yeast

A large pinch of salt

1 tablespoon vegetable or sunflower oil

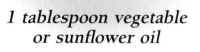

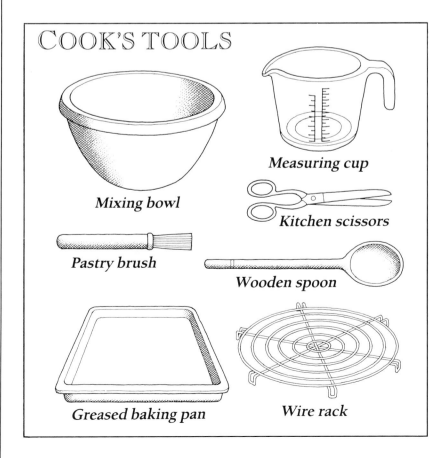

COOK'S TOOLS

Mixing bowl

Measuring cup

Kitchen scissors

Pastry brush

Wooden spoon

Greased baking pan

Wire rack

6 oz (¾ cup) warm water

*2⅔ cups
all-purpose
white flour*

Making the dough

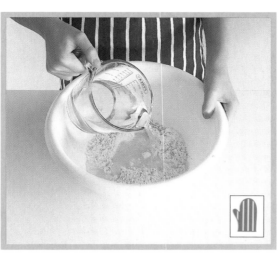

1 Preheat the oven to 450°F/
230°C. Put the flour, yeast, and
salt in the mixing bowl. Add the
vegetable oil and water.

2 Mix everything together into a
firm dough. If the dough is
sticky, add a little flour. Add a little
water if it is too dry.

3 Put the dough on a floured
table. Push your hands into the
dough, gather it into a ball, and turn
it again and again for 5 minutes.

4 Shape the dough into rolls (see
next page). Put them on the
greased baking pan. Cover loosely
with a dishtowel, then put them in
a warm place*.

5 When the rolls have doubled
in size, you can decorate them
however you want (see the next
page).

6 Bake them for 15 to 20 minutes.
They are done if they sound
hollow when tapped underneath.
Put them on the wire rack to cool.

TWIST AND ROLL

You can make bread rolls in all sorts of different shapes. You can vary them even more by using different seeds to make crunchy toppings.

To make the rolls, break the bread dough into eight pieces, all about the same size. Then follow the instructions on the right. Remember that the baked rolls will be twice as big as the dough, because they will grow when rising.

Decorating the rolls

When the rolls have risen and are ready to bake, you can decorate them with any of the things shown below. To give the rolls a golden brown glaze, you will also need a beaten egg and a pastry brush.

You will need

Sesame seeds

Caraway seeds

Poppy seeds

Raisins or currants

Brush the rolls lightly with the beaten egg. Sprinkle seeds over them and press gently into place. The rolls are now ready to go into the oven (see the previous page).

TORTOISE ROLL

Stick tiny balls of dough around a roll to look like four legs, a head, and a tail. Mark the top of the roll to look like a shell.

PRICKLY HEDGEHOG

Make a pointed snout shape at one end of a roll. Snip the rest of the roll, the hedgehog's body, with scissors to make prickles.

Flower roll sprinkled with caraway seeds

1 beaten egg

Prickly hedgehog with raisin eyes and nose

Cottage roll sprinkled with poppy seeds

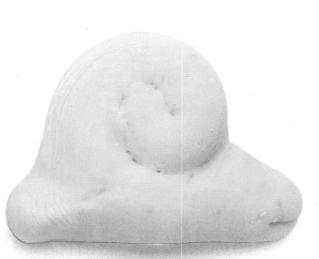

COTTAGE ROLL

Make a smaller ball of dough than the others. Brush the base of it with water. Stick it to a larger roll and make a dent in the top.

SNAIL ROLL

Roll a ball of dough into a sausage shape. Brush one side of it with water and wind it into a coil, leaving one end as the head.

FLOWER ROLL

Flatten a ball of dough slightly. Snip all round the edge of the dough with kitchen scissors to make petal shapes.

The finished rolls on a cooling rack

Bread Bears

You can make these bears using the recipe on page 28, but you need to double the ingredients given. You can also use a mixture of white and whole-wheat flour. When you have made the dough, break it into three different-sized balls, one for each bear. Apart from the dough, you will need decorating ingredients, a large, greased baking pan, and kitchen scissors or a knife.

You will need for decoration

Sesame seeds

Poppy seeds

1 beaten egg

Raisins or currants

Shredded cheese

Making the bears

1 Break a ball of dough in two. Roll half of it into a big ball for the bear's body. Put it on the baking pan and flatten it a little.

2 Break the remaining dough in two. Roll half of it into a small ball. Roll the other half into a sausage shape about 6 inches long.

3 Brush one side of the small ball with egg. Stick it to the bear's body, tucking it slightly underneath, to make the head.

4 Break off a piece of the sausage-shaped roll. Brush one side of it with egg and stick it to the bear's face. Pinch it into the shape of a snout.

5 Cut two small pieces for the ears and four bigger ones for the legs. Pinch them into position under the bear's body and head.

6 Using the kitchen scissors or a knife, snip or slash the ends of the bear's legs to make them look like paws with claws.

Letting the bears rise

7 Make all the bears this way. Cover them loosely with a dish towel and leave them in a warm place to rise for about an hour, until they have doubled in size. Then brush them lightly with beaten egg to glaze them and use raisins to make their eyes. Now you can add other decorations if you like.

Baking the bears

8 Bake the bears in the oven (see page 29) for about 25 minutes, depending on their size, until they are golden brown. Then put them on a wire rack to cool.

MOMMY BEAR

Raisins for eyes

Mommy bear was brushed with beaten egg and then sprinkled with sesame seeds.

DADDY BEAR

Raisins for eyes

BABY BEAR

Raisins for eyes

Daddy bear was brushed with beaten egg and then sprinkled with shredded cheese before being baked.

Baby bear was brushed with beaten egg and then decorated with poppy seeds.

PERFECT PASTRY

Here and on the next five pages you can find out how to make tiny tarts and quiches. These two pages show you how to make the pastry shells. The quantities will yield about thirty pastries, depending on the size of the pans you use. *Remember to have an adult handy for supervision while you are making this recipe.*

You will need

2 tablespoons (1 oz) sugar (for fruit tarts only)

About 3 tablespoons water

1 stick (4 oz) margarine or butter

A pinch of salt

1 cup (8 oz) all-purpose flour

COOK'S TOOLS

Mixing bowl

Knife

Fork

Rolling pin

Wooden spoon

Cookie cutter

Muffin pans or little tartlet pans

Wire rack

Making the pastry

1 Preheat the oven to 400°F/ 200°C. Put the flour, butter, and salt in the mixing bowl. Cut up the butter.

2 Rub the flour and butter together with your fingertips until they look like breadcrumbs. For fruit tarts, add the sugar.

3 Now mix in the water, a little at a time. You should have a soft ball of dough that leaves the sides of the bowl clean.

4 Sprinkle flour on the table and your rolling pin. Put the dough on the table and roll it out until it is quite thin.

5 Cut circles out of the pastry, using a cookie cutter or cup. The circles should be a bit bigger than your tart pans.

6 Lay each circle of pastry over a pan. Gather in the edges and press the pastry into place so that it fits the pan.

For fruit tarts

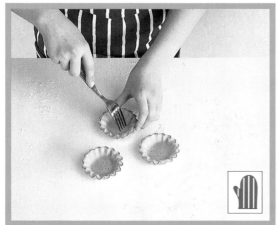

7 Prick the bases of the pastry shells with a fork. Put them in the oven and bake them for 15 minutes, until golden brown.

8 Let the pans cool, then pry the pastry shells out with a knife and put them on a wire rack. See how to fill them on pages 36 to 37.

For little quiches

9 Add the filling now (see pages 38–39). Then put the quiches in the oven to bake for about 20 minutes, until the filling sets.

Turn to the next four pages for filling ideas. 35

FRUIT TARTS

To make these fruit tarts, bake the pastry shells first (see the previous page). Then fill them with fruit and glaze them with melted jam. It is best to use soft fruits like those shown below, because you don't have to cook them.

You will need

2¼ cups (1 lb) fruit, such as:

Baked, sweet pastry shells

Fresh or canned pineapple slices

Raspberries

Blackberries

Seedless grapes

COOK'S TOOLS

Wooden spoon

Small saucepan

Sharp knife

Pastry brush

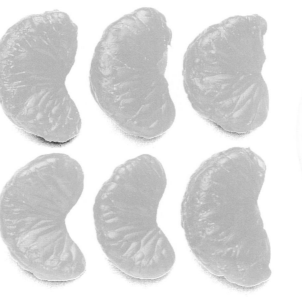

Canned mandarin orange sections

½ cup (4 oz) clear red jelly or strained apricot jam

Filling the tarts

1 Make a glaze for the tarts by melting the clear red jelly or strained apricot jam in the small saucepan over a low heat.

2 Brush the insides of the pastry shells with the glaze. Wash the fresh fruit and drain the canned fruit. Cut the grapes in half.

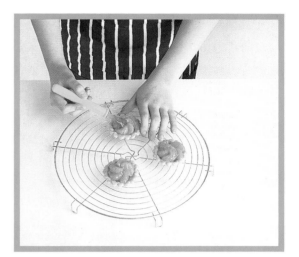

3 Arrange the fruit in the pastry shells, as shown below. Then brush the fruit with the glaze, which will set as it cools.

The finished tarts

Arrange mandarin orange sections so they overlap to form a circle.

This tart has a ring of blackberries with a raspberry in the center.

Use slivers of grape, four pineapple slices and a grape for the center.

Use pineapple slices, orange sections, raspberries, and halved grapes.

The grape in the center of this is put between two chunks of pineapple.

This one has mandarin orange sections and blackberries.

37

MINI QUICHES

When making quiches or nondessert tarts, put the filling in the pastry shells before you cook them. You can add whatever you want to the basic filling of eggs and milk to give the quiches any flavor you like. Try combinations of the filling ingredients shown below.

You will need

2 eggs

⅔ cup milk

Unbaked, unsweetened pastry shells (see pages 34–35)

Plus any of these ingredients

Chopped scallions

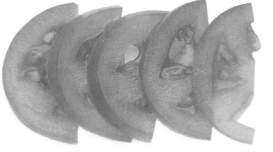
Sliced tomatoes

Strips of sliced ham

Finely sliced leeks

Sliced mushrooms

Canned tuna fish

Shredded cheese

COOK'S TOOLS

Knife

Fork

Cheese grater

Cutting board

Measuring cup

38

What you do

1 Slice the tomatoes, the scallions, and mushrooms. Cut the ham into strips. Drain the tuna. Shred the cheese.

2 Break the eggs into the measuring cup. Beat them well with the fork. Pour in the milk and whisk the mixture together.

3 Arrange the fillings in the pastry shells, pour the egg mixture over the fillings. Put them in the oven for 20 minutes (see page 35).

The finished quiches

This quiche is filled with a mixture of tuna fish and scallions.

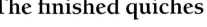

Place sliced leeks in this quiche. Then put strips of ham on top.

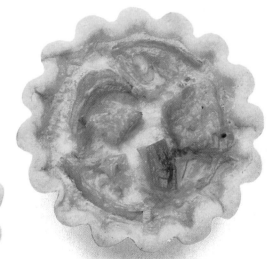

Tuna fish and sliced tomatoes are used in this quiche.

This quiche has shredded cheese topped with sliced tomatoes.

In this quiche, sliced mushrooms are arranged to overlap slightly.

39

CHOCOLATE DIPS

You can make delicious homemade candy by dipping your favorite fruits and nuts into melted chocolate. Make candy out of the things shown below and put them in pretty paper cups to give away as presents. You can also use them to decorate a special cake, or best of all – just enjoy eating them! *Remember to have an adult handy for supervision while you are making this recipe.*

You will need

6 ounces dark chocolate

Cherries

Fresh mandarin orange sections

Brazil nuts

Blanched almonds

Walnuts

COOK'S TOOLS

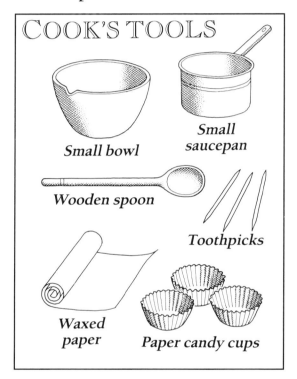

Small bowl

Small saucepan

Wooden spoon

Toothpicks

Waxed paper

Paper candy cups

Melting the chocolate

1 Break up the chocolate into a bowl. Heat some water in the saucepan over a low heat until it just begins to bubble.

2 Keeping the heat on low, place the bowl over the saucepan. Stir the chocolate with a wooden spoon until it completely melts.

3 Turn off the heat. Very carefully move the saucepan and the bowl from the stove to a mat or dish towel.

Strawberries

Seedless grapes

Dipping the fruit and nuts

4 One at a time, put a piece of fruit on a toothpick and dip half of it into the chocolate. Then put it on waxed paper to dry.

5 Using your fingers, dip the nuts halfway into the melted chocolate, one at a time. Let them dry on the waxed paper.

Arranging your candies

You can put the finished candies in paper candy cups. If they are for a special occasion, arrange them in circular patterns on a large plate.

SURPRISE CAKE

For birthdays, parties, and other celebrations,
it is fun to make a special cake. Or you can
make a cake just because you want to give
someone a nice surprise. Here is a recipe
for a light and delicious yellow cake that
you can decorate however you like.
You can find out how to make the cake
below. Then turn to the next four
pages to see how to ice and decorate it
in different ways. *Remember to have
an adult handy for supervision
while you are making this recipe.*

You will need

1½ sticks (6 oz) softened butter

1⅓ cups all-purpose flour

Making the cake

1 Preheat the oven to 350°F/
180°C. Grease the pans
thoroughly with some of the
butter.

2 Put the softened butter and
sugar in the mixing bowl. Beat
them with the wooden spoon until
the mixture is pale and creamy.

3 Beat the eggs in a small bowl.
Add them to the butter-and-
sugar mixture a little at a time,
stirring in well until it is smooth.

3 eggs

¾ cup (6 oz) sugar

COOK'S TOOLS

Mixing bowl

Fork

Wooden spoon

2 8-inch
layer cake pans

Small bowl

2 wire racks

1½ teaspoons baking powder

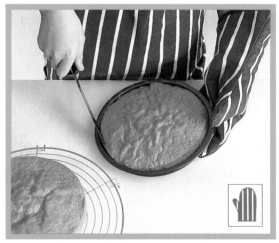

4 Sift the flour and baking powder into the wet ingredients and beat well. The batter should be soft and light.

5 Pour half of the batter into each pan and level it. Place the pans in the oven for 20 to 25 minutes.

6 The layers are done when well-risen and brown. They should feel springy in the middle. Turn them out onto wire racks to cool.

Now turn the page.

43

CANDY CAKE

This cake is filled and topped with chocolate buttercream icing and fancifully decorated. Copy the Candy-nut Hen, or make up a new picture.

You will need

1 tablespoon (½ oz) cocoa powder

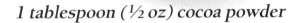

6 tablespoons (3 oz) softened butter

1–2 tablespoons milk

COOK'S TOOLS

Strainer

Mixing bowl

Knife

Wooden spoon

¾ cup (6 oz) confectioners' sugar

Icing the cake

1 Put the butter in the bowl and cut into small pieces. Beat hard with the wooden spoon and stir until the butter is soft and creamy.

2 Sift the sugar and cocoa powder into the bowl a little at a time, mixing well with the butter. Then stir in the milk.

3 When the layers are cool, spread half the icing on one of them. Put the other cake on top and spread the rest of the icing over it.

44

Turn the page for another decorated cake.

Arranging the Candy-nut Hen

4 Now decorate the cake. Press the candy firmly into the icing. Start with the border, do the nest next, and arrange the hen last of all.

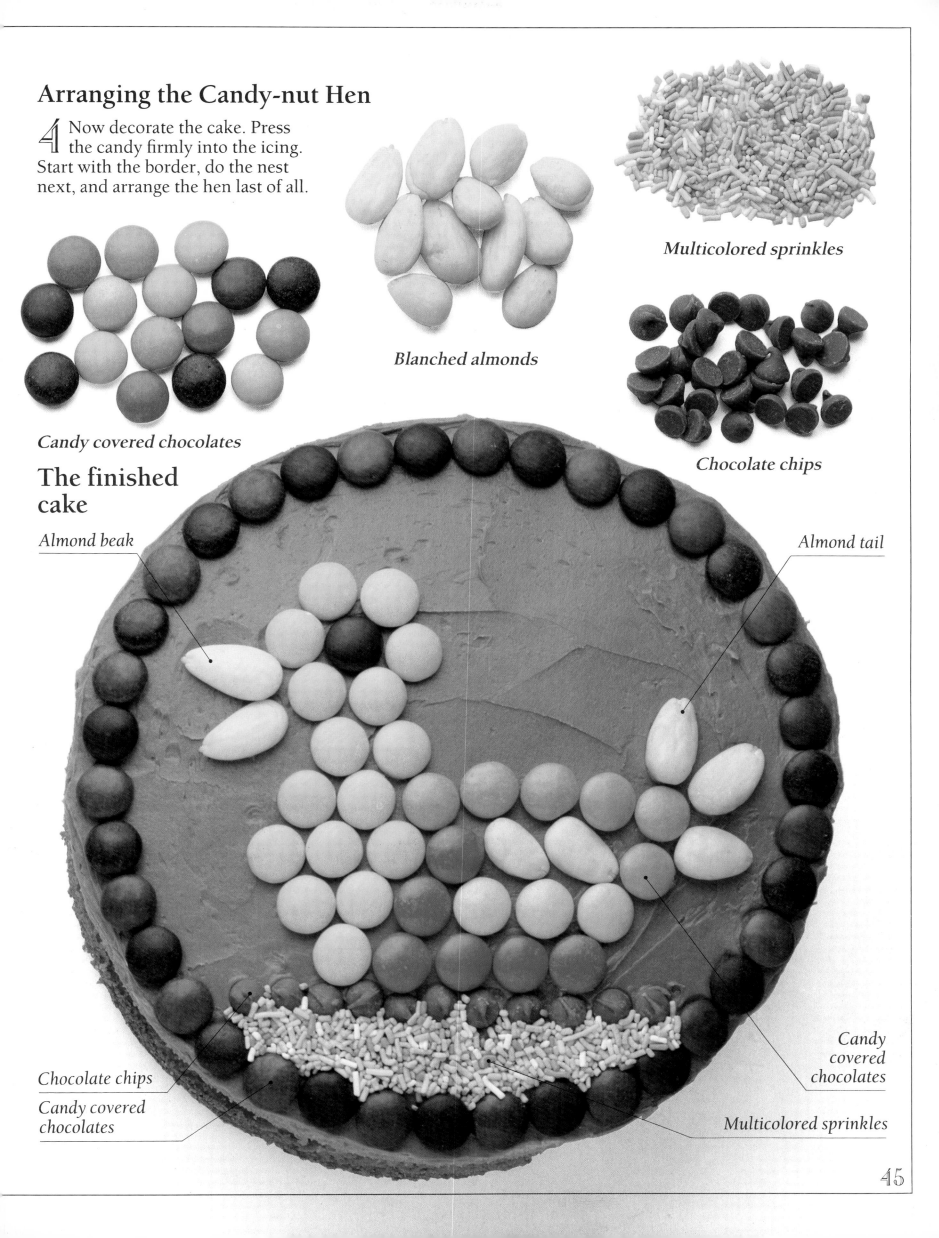

Multicolored sprinkles

Blanched almonds

Candy covered chocolates

Chocolate chips

The finished cake

Almond beak

Almond tail

Chocolate chips

Candy covered chocolates

Candy covered chocolates

Multicolored sprinkles

45

FROSTED FLOWER CAKE

This cake is filled with jam and topped with icing and crystallized grapes and flowers. We have used rose petals, but you can use any small flowers if they are safe to eat, (ask your parents first). The flowers and fruit take 2 to 3 hours to dry, so allow time.

You will need

1 egg

**White icing, using 1⅔ cups confectioners' sugar and 3 tablespoons of hot water

What to do

1 Crack the egg over a bowl. Slip the yolk from one half of the shell to the other, so that the white slips into the bowl.

2 Whisk the egg white until it is frothy. On a wire rack placed over a plate, paint the rose petals and grapes with egg white.

3 Sprinkle sugar over the rose petals. Dip the grapes into the sugar to coat them. Then leave the rose petals and grapes to drain.

COOK'S TOOLS

Pastry brush

Teaspoon

2 bowls

Knife

Whisk

Wire rack

4 Spread each cake with jam and sandwich them together. Make the icing and spread it over the top of the cake, with a wet knife.

5 Arrange the rose petals and grapes on the cake before the icing sets. They will stick to the cake as the icing dries.

**Using these measurements, follow instructions for making plain white icing on page 14.

Bowl of sugar

Rose petals or small flowers

Grapes

Apricot jam

The finished cake

Crystallized grapes

Crystallized petals

Crystallized petals

CHOCOLATE TRUFFLES

The amounts of the ingredients shown make about eight gooey, delicious truffles, so double or triple the recipe to make more. *If you plan to chop the nuts yourself, remember to ask an adult to help you.*

You will need

¼ cup
cocoa powder

(powdered) ½ cup confectioners' sugar

¼ cup (2 oz) chopped nuts

¼ cup (2 oz) cream cheese

Chocolate sprinkles

What to do

1 Put the cheese, chopped nuts, confectioners' sugar, and cocoa powder in the mixing bowl and stir until everything is well mixed.

2 Now roll the mixture into marble-size balls in the palms of your hands. You can make them bigger if you like.

Rolling the truffles

3 Spread the sprinkles on the work surface and carefully roll the truffles in them. Then put each one in a paper candy cup.

The finished truffles

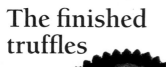